HEAVEN ON EARTH
Studies in Matthew

TOGETHER IN FAITH SERIES
Learner Session Guide

Janelle Rozek Hooper

AUGSBURG FORTRESS

HEAVEN ON EARTH: STUDIES IN MATTHEW
Learner Session Guide

Together in Faith Series
Book of Faith Adult Bible Studies

Copyright © 2010 Augsburg Fortress. All rights reserved. Except for brief quotations in critical articles or reviews, no part of this book may be reproduced in any manner without prior written permission from the publisher. For more information, visit: www.augsburgfortress.org/copyrights or write to: Permissions, Augsburg Fortress, Box 1209, Minneapolis, MN 55440-1209.

 Book of Faith is an initiative of the
Evangelical Lutheran Church in America
God's work. Our hands.

For more information about the Book of Faith initiative, go to www.bookoffaith.org.

Scripture quotations, unless otherwise marked, are from New Revised Standard Version Bible, copyright © 1989 Division of Christian Education of the National Council of Churches of Christ in the United States of America. Used by permission. All rights reserved.

Web site addresses are provided in this resource for your use. These listings do not represent an endorsement of the sites by Augsburg Fortress, nor do we vouch for their content for the life of this resource.

ISBN: 9781451401226
Writer: Janelle Rozek Hooper
Cover and interior design: Spunk Design Machine, spkdm.com
Typesetting: PerfecType, Nashville, TN

The paper used in this publication meets the minimum requirements of American National Standard for Information Sciences—Permanence of Paper for Printed Library Materials, ANSI Z329.48-1984.

Manufactured in the U.S.A.
14 13 12 11 10   1 2 3 4 5 6 7 8 9 10

CONTENTS

1 Who wants heaven on earth? — 5
Matthew 4:12-23 (Year A—Third Sunday after Epiphany)

2 What does the kingdom of heaven have to do with us? — 12
Matthew 5:1-12 (Year A—Fourth Sunday after Epiphany)

3 Are we the right ones to bring heaven to earth? — 18
Matthew 5:13-20 (Year A—Fifth Sunday after Epiphany)

4 If this is heaven on earth, what's up with all the laws? — 25
Matthew 5:21-37 (Year A—Sixth Sunday after Epiphany)

5 Bringing heaven to earth sounds hard—do we have what it takes? — 32
Matthew 5:38-48 (Year A—Seventh Sunday after Epiphany)

6 Will you trust God for help in bringing heaven to earth? — 39
Matthew 6:24-34 (Year A—Eighth Sunday after Epiphany)

SESSION ONE

Matthew 4:12-23

Learner Session Guide

 Focus Statement

Now is the time for us to follow in Jesus' footsteps and bring heaven to earth.

 Key Verse

Immediately they . . . followed (Jesus). Matthew 4:20

Who wants heaven on earth?

 Focus Image

Where might that be? © Image Source / SuperStock

Gather

Check-in

Welcome! Take this time to connect or reconnect with the others in your group.

Pray

God, Creator of heaven and earth, we want to know you more. Unveil our eyes. Open our hearts. Create in us a deeper understanding of what it means to experience heaven on earth. In Jesus' name we pray. Amen.

Focus Activity

Get to know the other people in your group by talking about your life circumstances—what is going on with you "right now." In today's session, we learn that now is the time for the kingdom of heaven—that it is not far from us, but nearer than we think. How does today's Focus Image speak to this?

SESSION ONE

 Notes

Open Scripture
Read Matthew 4:12-23.

- How does the mention of John the Baptizer's arrest at the beginning of this text make you feel?

- In Matthew 4:15-16, we hear about how Jesus is fulfilling prophecy. Why is this important?

- Jesus' first ministry words are, "Repent, for the kingdom of heaven has come near" (4:17). Why do you think he chose these words to start his ministry? What are some other phrases you think Jesus could have used?

Join the Conversation
Historical Context

In Jesus' day, one-third of the children died before the age of six. "By the mid-teens, 60 percent would have died. By the mid-twenties, 75 percent were dead and by the mid-forties, the figure reached 90 percent. Perhaps 3 percent of the population made it to their sixties. Few ordinary people lived out their thirties . . . moreover, it is obvious that much of Jesus' audience would have been younger than he . . ." (*Social-Science Commentary on the Synoptic Gospels* (*SSCG*) by Bruce J. Malina and Richard L. Rohrbaugh, [Fortress Press, 2003], p. 327).

1. Matthew 4:12 in the New Revised Standard Version begins with a word that suggests "there's no time like the present."
- What is that word?
- Note that Jesus "started" his ministry when he was 30. What does it mean to you that Jesus starts his ministry in his "senior years"?

2. Given the severe conditions of life in Jesus' day, what would you have considered to be "good news/bad news"? Matthew purposefully uses the specific term "good news" because it was a political term of

SESSION ONE

 Notes

the day. Chapter 4 verse 23 is the first time in Matthew we hear the words "good news." Look at the previous chapters with:
- Mary's unexpected pregnancy and Joseph's near dismissal (1:18-25).
- The Magi's dream warning them about Herod (2:1-12).
- Mary, Joseph, and Jesus fleeing for their lives to Egypt (2:13-15).
- The massacre of infants and their making a home in Nazareth (2:16-23).
- The devil tempting Jesus (4:1-11).

In light of all this "bad news", how do you see the "now" of Matthew 4:12 as being the right time to hear "good news"?

3. Let's talk about . . . fishermen. What kind of people were they? What was their status? What were their responsibilities? Did the kingdom of heaven coming near to fishermen simply mean more fish? That might seem heavenly to some anglers, but what about Simon Peter? Compare Peter's first fishing encounter with Jesus (Luke 5:1-11) to one he had after the resurrection (John 21).

Literary Context

Look at the action words in today's text, as they paint a vivid picture for us. We see the words "immediately" and "followed" used twice. Repetition was one of the ways writers emphasized things before the days of punctuation! In addition, we hear about Jesus curing and healing "every" body. All of this speaks to the hyperbolic force of Matthew's message.

1. Do you think the fishermen left "immediately," no questions asked? Would you need to ask questions before you "left everything behind"? What would they be?

2. Do you think "every" single person was healed, or that the mention of "everybody" was a figure of speech for Jesus' attraction and power? Could it be a common exaggeration similar to what we still use today, like "everyone is doing it"? Why might Matthew use exaggerated generalizations to talk about the "kingdom of heaven"?

3. When Jesus says in verse 19, "I will make you fish for people," it is commonly thought that Jesus means they will fish for people. How does it change your idea of what it means to be a disciple if you are "fishing" or if you are "the fish"? Respond to the phrase: "Christianity is caught, not taught."

SESSION ONE

 Notes

Lutheran Context

Lutherans do not focus on salvation as a one-time commitment to God that saves us from hell. Throughout Matthew, starting in today's text, verse 23, Jesus heals and cures people, thus "saving them," which is not limited to saving them from hell and providing them with eternal life.

1. How does this Lutheran understanding of wholeness inform our understanding of what "heaven on earth" looks like?

2. According to Luther, baptism is not merely a ritual that happens in our past or something that gives hope for our future; it's God's constant promise that "daily a new person can come forth and rise up to live before God in righteousness and purity forever" (*ELW*, p. 1165). How would it affect the decisions you make on a daily basis to be soaked in your baptismal promises rather than worried about making "right or wrong decisions" leading to heaven or hell?

- How is this similar to/different from the other Gospels? See Luke 4:40-44; Mark 10:13-16, 23-27; John 3:1-6.
- How is this similar to/different from what we find in the epistles? See Romans 14:17; 1 Corinthians 4:20; Galatians 5:19-25.

From what you've gathered from these passages, imagine together what the kingdom of heaven on earth should be like. How does it compare to kingdoms of the earth?

Devotional Context

"Prophets read hearts, not cards or crystal balls or configurations in the heavens. What is in the human heart they compare to what is in the mind of God. The contrast becomes prophecy" (Joan Chittister from *Liguorian* magazine, www.liguorian.org).

1. What do you think of Joan Chittister's definition of a prophet/prophecy? How does it compare to your picture of a prophet (what do they look like, what do they say)?

2. Although we talk about Jesus as the "fulfillment of prophecy" we do not always refer to him as "Jesus the prophet." What characteristics of the prophet Jesus are similar to Deborah (Judges 4–5), Elijah (1 Kings 17), Moses (Exodus 32), or Anna (Luke 2:36-38)?

SESSION ONE

3. It is tricky finding a balance in our lives and figuring out when and how to follow Jesus. When and why would we "drop everything"? Consider by way of a modern example the story of Greg Mortenson. In his best-selling book *Three Cups of Tea* (Penguin Books, 2006), Mortenson describes his willingness to live out of his car, keep his belongings in a storage unit, shower at the gym, and work the holiday/weekend/night shifts as a nurse in order to have the flexibility to go mountain-climbing. When his attempt to reach the summit of K2 (one of the highest peaks in the world) fails, he literally stumbles into a Pakistani camp where the direction of his life changes. From then on, Mortenson finds a calling in his life beyond climbing physical mountains to climbing the steep mountain of fighting terrorism by providing schools in rural poor communities in Pakistan.

- How did the "flexibility" of Mortenson's life prepare him for this calling?
- What role does divine "serendipity" play in bringing the kingdom of heaven near to earth?
- Can you see your church welcoming the help of other religious groups who are also working towards heaven on earth?
- If someone came to our place of work and asked us to quit our jobs right then and there to do mission work, if the seed had been planted in our hearts, might it be possible that we also "immediately" follow?
- Is there a way to use our current life circumstances to stay where we are at and still follow faithfully?

Wrap-up

Be ready to look back over the work your group has done in this session.

Pray

Holy Spirit, come. Come into our lives this week ahead, and point out to us places of heaven on earth. Holy Spirit, guide our words, our thoughts, and our actions as we seek to follow you. In Jesus' name we pray. Amen.

Notes

SESSION ONE

Notes

Extending the Conversation

Homework

1. In Scripture it says "prophecy is a gift" (1 Corinthians 14:1), but it's not a gift we usually talk about in the Lutheran church. Is there a time you thought your church was being prophetic?

2. The prophet Jesus doesn't collect a paycheck (neither do other biblical prophets as far as we know). What do you think is the correlation between the fishermen also "leaving everything" to follow the prophet Jesus? Is it possible to be prophetic and garner a paycheck? Ask your pastor for their opinion on this. Share their point of view with your group.

3. Ask your friends or family what comes to mind when people think of "heaven on earth" (for example, a Hawaiian paradise or Jewish, Christian, and Muslim neighbors getting along). Be prepared to bring a picture or written results of what you find to share with the group next week.

Enrichment

1. Do some research into the lives of the prophets and prophetesses. Select a major or minor prophet from the Old Testament based on their books in the Bible's table of contents. Learn more about the prophetesses: Miriam, Deborah, Huldah, Noadiah, and Anna. Don't forget to check out John the Baptizer and the mysterious New Testament prophet, Agabus! Perhaps each member of the group can offer a brief biography of their prophet of choice over the weeks of this unit. Be sure to focus on how these prophets served to bring heaven on earth.

2. Read pages 777–780 of *Harry Potter and the Order of the Phoenix* by J.K. Rowling (Arthur A Levine Books, 2003) or watch the scene in the movie that recounts Harry's experience in the hall of prophecy. What cultural perceptions of prophets/prophecy are found here?

3. Listen to or read the words to the song "Come, Now Is the Time to Worship" by Brian Doerksen (emphasis on the word "Now"!). Many online music videos can be found such as the one at http://www.youtube.com/watch?v=K8kRHAITTD0.

SESSION ONE

For Further Reading

The Cry of the Prophet: A Call to Fullness of Life by Joan Chittister (Benetvision, 2009). Sister Joan Chittister searches Scripture to show us what we have in common with the great biblical prophets. She also speaks about the role of prophecy in our world, insisting that prophecy is not a luxury but rather an essential dimension of the Christian life.

Three Cups of Tea by Greg Mortenson and David Oliver Relin (Penguin Books, 2006). This book is an example of some Muslim leaders welcoming, even protecting, Greg Mortenson (who was raised Lutheran) as he works to provide schools for the poorest and most rural areas of Pakistan.

Available at www.augsburgfortress.org/store:

Baptized, We Live: Lutheranism as a Way of Life by Daniel Erlander (Augsburg Fortress, 1995). A graphically refreshing description of Lutheranism as a way of seeing, hearing, teaching, and following.

The Message and the Kingdom: How Jesus & Paul Ignited a Revolution & Transformed the Ancient World by Richard A. Horsley and Neil Asher Silberman (Fortress Press, 2002). Horsley and Silberman demonstrate how the quest for the kingdom of God by Jesus, Paul, and the earliest churches should be understood as both a spiritual journey and a political response to the "mindless acts of violence, inequality, and injustice that characterized the kings of men."

Social-Science Commentary on the Synoptic Gospels by Bruce J. Malina and Richard L. Rohrbaugh (Fortress Press, 2003). An examination of each unit in the Synoptics, employing methodologies of cultural anthropology, macro-sociology, and social psychology.

Notes

SESSION TWO

Matthew 5:1-12

Learner Session Guide

Focus Statement
By belonging to God we are blessed to be a part of bringing heaven to earth.

Key Verse
For theirs is the kingdom of heaven. Matthew 5:3

What does the kingdom of heaven have to do with us?

Focus Image

Are "The Beatitudes" the key to the kingdom of heaven on earth? © RubberBall / SuperStock

Gather

Check-in
Welcome! Take this time to connect or reconnect with the others in your group. Be ready to share new thoughts or insights about your last session.

Pray
Jesus, you bless us with a living example of what it means to bring heaven to earth. Give us courageous hearts today to ask the tough questions about what the kingdom of heaven has to do with us. We ask all this in your holy nam. Amen.

Focus Activity
The Beatitudes are very popular, probably because both the Greek and Hebrew words for "blessed" can also be translated as "happy."

Heaven on Earth Learner Guide

SESSION TWO

- Make a quick list of three things you are happy about and share with your group.
- Do the Beatitudes bring to mind a specific memory or image for you?
- How does the Focus Image relate to this discussion about happiness?

Open Scripture
Read Matthew 5:1-12.

- How would you define the words "heaven," "earth," and "righteousness"? Ponder the link between these words and how they play off of each other.

- Do you feel the passages suggest that "heaven on earth" is related to being successful?

- How would the Beatitudes speak to an oppressed people?

Join the Conversation
Historical Context

The author of Matthew considered Mark's Gospel inadequate and may have even intended for Matthew to replace Mark's Gospel. Matthew didn't see in Mark's Gospel any expectations of how to be the church in community, which was highly important to this Gospel writer.

1. Since Luke and Matthew both use Mark as a source for their writing, take a look at the similarities between Matthew's "Sermon on the Mount" and Luke's "Sermon on the Plain" (6:20-26). In what ways does Matthew's wording showcase the kingdom of heaven as the work of the church in community?

2. The time in which Jesus lived and the book of Matthew was written (as much as 70 years later) was predominantly an "honor-shame" culture. The Beatitudes with their "Blessed are . . ." can be understood as "How honorable are . . ." as would have been very familiar to the people living in this type of society.

Notes

SESSION TWO

Notes

- Now compare the Beatitudes with Matthew 23:13-35. Look at these two texts and note the "honor attributes" and "shame accusations" (*Social-Science Commentary on the Synoptic Gospels* by Bruce J. Malina and Richard L. Rohrbaugh [Fortress Press, 2003], p. 47).
- What do you think are the overarching reasons behind the "blessings" or the "woes" in these passages?
- Do you believe that Jesus promotes an "honor-shame" culture? How do these passages shape your vision of Jesus and what the kingdom of heaven has to do with us today?

Literary Context

The term "the beatitudes" entered our modern vocabulary by means of the Bible; however it is not unique to Jesus or Matthew. "Beatitudes" is a literary expression, derived from Latin, for a catalog of blessings. But it was a genre that was also used by Jewish writers (Deuteronomy 28) and "pagan" literature that was certainly familiar to the writer of Matthew. In the Hebrew Bible, this term is used in two particular ways. In the Wisdom tradition it is used to express the fortunate position of people in their current situation. In the Prophets, beatitudes express a "future blessedness for those who are presently in dire circumstances, but who will be vindicated" when the kingdom of heaven becomes a reality on earth (*The New Interpreter's Bible*, Volume VIII [Abingdon Press, 1995], p. 177).

1. Look at each of the beatitudes in Matthew 5 and discuss where (by way of an "X") you would place the realization of that blessing on a range between your current situation (Here-and-Now) and your hopes for the future (Here-Ever-After).

Vs. 3	Here-and-Now ————————	Here-Ever-After
Vs. 4	Here-and-Now ————————	Here-Ever-After
Vs. 5	Here-and-Now ————————	Here-Ever-After
Vs. 6	Here-and-Now ————————	Here-Ever-After
Vs. 7	Here-and-Now ————————	Here-Ever-After
Vs. 8	Here-and-Now ————————	Here-Ever-After
Vs. 9	Here-and-Now ————————	Here-Ever-After
Vs. 10	Here-and-Now ————————	Here-Ever-After
Vs. 11	Here-and-Now ————————	Here-Ever-After

2. Focus on the second half of each beatitude. How have Christians utilized those promises to form their expression of the good news to the world? How do the Beatitudes continue the prophetic tradition as a way of describing a church community that's concerned with the idea of "heaven on earth"?

SESSION TWO

3. It is thought that the Beatitudes are the first in a compilation of a number of Jesus' sermons.

- Scan Matthew 5–7. How does it "read" to you all at once?
- What do you think Matthew might be trying to accomplish by putting these sermons all together?

Lutheran Context

Have you ever noticed that images of "heaven on earth" are often pictures of serene-looking places, without a human anywhere to be seen? These are beautiful places where we can "get away" from other people, from work, from the phone, or from any other distraction that is the opposite of what Jesus means by the "kingdom of heaven." The kingdom of heaven is about people; it is about work; it is about communities, neighborhoods, the "messy" places where our lives intersect, and how these can become places of welcome, neighborliness, justice, and peace.

1. Use some paper and sketch a scene of people doing God's work, creating heaven on earth, and share with each other.

We understand Luther's dying words to be, "We are beggars, this is true." While having a healthy grasp of what it means to "fear God," Luther certainly did not lack confidence in what he believed and yet retained humbleness in his relationship to God. Matthew also conveys humbleness or "meekness," which is an essential aspect of the Christian life. This meekness is not about being a doormat for others to walk on—but rather extravagantly compassionate and generous, grounded in the confidence of what one believes and to whom one belongs.

2. The Sermon on the Mount, and the Beatitudes in particular, contain heavenly wisdom that seems foolish on earth. Does a world where people are "foolishly" generous to one another (without being less of oneself), sound like "heaven on earth" to you? Make a list of people who represent "heaven on earth" to you.

Devotional Context

The Beatitudes are not merely statements about how individuals are supposed to act in order to create the kingdom of heaven in their own lives. The Beatitudes are how entire Christian communities are called to make the kingdom of heaven a reality for everyone (from *NIB*, p. 178).

 Notes

SESSION TWO

Notes

1. Sing or read the song "O for a World" by Sister Miriam Therese Winter. How does this song depict the kingdom of heaven? How would you feel singing this song in worship?

> *O for a world where everyone respects each other's ways,*
> *Where love is lived and all is done with justice and praise.*
>
> *O for a world where goods are shared and misery relieved,*
> *Where truth is spoken, children spared, equality achieved.*
>
> *We welcome one world family and struggle with each voice,*
> *That opens us to unity and gives our vision voice.*
>
> *The poor are rich, the weak are strong, the foolish ones are wise.*
> *Tell all who mourn: outcasts belong, who perishes will arise.*
>
> *O for a world preparing for God's glorious reign of peace,*
> *Where time and tears will be no more, and all but love will cease.*
>
> Copyright © Medical Mission Sisters, 1990. Used by permission.

2. Discuss the meaning of this statement: *We create "heaven on earth" as we are living out the Beatitudes in community.*

3. Knowing that the "kingdom of heaven" is a group effort, how does that change the way you think of it, your interest in creating it, or how you fit into it?

Wrap-up

Be ready to look back over the work your group has done in this session.

Pray

Holy One, our lives are full to overflowing the more we follow you. Give us a vision of the kingdom of heaven that we might eagerly be a part of it. All this we ask in your holy name. Amen.

Extending the Conversation

Homework

1. Read the next session's Bible text, Matthew 5:13-20, and come with thoughts and questions for conversation.

2. Ask around, Christian and non-Christian friends alike, what comes to mind when they hear "Beatitudes" or "Sermon on the Mount." Share your findings with your group next week.

3. Write your own song or poem to the tune of "Oh, for a Thousand Tongues to Sing" (*ELW* 886) that would depict heaven on earth.

SESSION TWO

Enrichment

1. Watch the clip from the movie *The Nativity Story* (New Line Cinema, 2006) where the Romans come to Mary's town and force her father to give up his donkey. This shows how real Roman occupation and the tenant/owner relationship weighed daily on people's lives.

2. Talk with your pastor about his or her thoughts regarding this text, including how he or she has preached it and what it means to him or her. Take notes, with your pastor's permission, and share it with the group.

3. Plan a "Heaven on Earth Day" in which your group can lead your congregation to realize the Beatitudes of Matthew 5 in tangible and creative ways. For example: Verse 3—coming to a better understanding about homelessness (www.endhomelessness.org/files/1155_file_Lifetime_WS.pdf); Verse 4—giving comfort to the bereaved through art (http://www.recover-from-grief.com/creativity-grief.html); Verse 5—offering a Christian wills awareness seminar; and so on.

For Further Reading

Available at www.augsburgfortress.org/store:

Amazing Grace: A Vocabulary of Faith by Kathleen Norris (Riverhead Books, 1998). Read especially her encounter with the Beatitudes on page 149.

The New Interpreter's Bible: A Commentary in Twelve Volumes, Volume VIII (Abingdon Press, 1995). See if your pastor or church library will let you borrow this volume so you can read the "Excursus: Kingdom of Heaven in Matthew" on pages 288-294.

Speaking of Trust: Conversing with Luther about the Sermon on the Mount by Dr. Martin E. Marty (Augsburg Fortress, 2003). This title in the "Lutheran Voices" series brings together passages from Luther's preaching on the Sermon on the Mount and Marty's comments about the place of trust in the life of faith.

Notes

SESSION THREE

Matthew 5:13-20

Learner Session Guide

Are we the right ones to bring heaven to earth?

 Focus Image

How full is your shaker? © Bruce Yuan-Yue Bi PCL / SuperStock

 Focus Statement

Not only are we the people to help bring heaven to earth, but we are to teach others to do the same.

 Key Verse

Therefore, whoever breaks one of the least of these commandments, and teaches others to do the same, will be called least in the kingdom of heaven; but whoever does them and teaches them will be called great in the kingdom of heaven. Matthew 5:19

Gather

Check-in

Welcome! Take this time to connect or reconnect with the others in your group. Be ready to share new thoughts or insights about your last session.

Pray

Jesus, you not only tell us, but show us what is possible. Give me the courage in this space, and amidst these people, to open myself to your guidance so that we might find ourselves intrigued, curious, and in awe of the possibility of heaven on earth. In your holy name we pray. Amen.

Focus Activity

Jesus is telling us we belong to the community of people that are responsible for bringing heaven to earth. What kind of things have you wanted to be a part of in your life? Recall a time when you

SESSION THREE

really wanted to be a part of something, how you felt, and what really sold you on it. Share briefly with your group.

Open Scripture
Read Matthew 5:13-20.

- What word(s) caught your attention? Why?

- Highlight in your Bibles or keep tabs in your learner book how many times the word "heaven" is used in these verses. If you have not already, now might be a good time to discuss different people's points of view about heaven.

- Have you ever felt like an instrument of God's, helping to bring heaven to earth?

Join the Conversation
Historical Context

Salt used to be an extremely valuable spice. These days salt comes so cheap at the grocery store we think nothing of using it. Among the first century hearers of this Gospel, women who worked to prepare meals would have particularly taken notice of his use of metaphor about salt. Homes of this time were often a single room that contained a "kitchen" composed of an earthen oven, a double stove, a millstone for grinding, and a dung heap. The earthen stove used the dung heap for fuel. The dung heap was salted as a catalyst to make the dung burn (*Social-Science Commentary on the Synoptic Gospels* by Bruce J. Malina and Richard L. Rohrbaugh [Fortress Press, 2003], p. 50). Few of us today are familiar with "salt that has lost its taste." In the end, salt loses its saltiness when it can't even serve to facilitate burning. Salt that was no longer good for cooking, either in the food or as a fuel additive, was an understandable reality for Matthew's audience.

1. Read Matthew 5:13. In what ways does Jesus' metaphor still manage to speak to us? Brainstorm uses for salt and how those uses serve as a metaphor of the church. Be creative!

Notes

SESSION THREE

 Notes

2. If you were to talk about what it would be like for Christians to lose their capacity for bringing heaven to earth, what kind of other comparisons could you make using ordinary objects like salt?

3. Read Matthew 5:14-16. It was common for these one-room houses to burn oil in lamps for a meager source of light. In order to put out the oil fire without causing lots of smoke, the fire was put under a bushel (*SSCG*, p. 51).
- What would be a modern-day equivalent of "hiding our light under a bushel?"
- How is choosing not to shine our light a decision not to help bring heaven to earth?

Literary Context

As we've just seen, both the Old and New Testaments regularly use metaphor. Whether it is referring to people as "salt" and "light" or calling God our "shield" (Psalm 3:3) and thinking of Jesus as a mother "hen" (Luke 13:34), these figures of speech help make profound spiritual concepts easier for people to understand.

1. Try to think of common items in your home and how they could be used to talk about God. For example, in what ways is a bed comforter like the Holy Spirit as "Comforter" (John 15:26 KJV)?

2. Jesus, by way of Matthew, understands the pull of our emotions and attitudes on the daily choices we make. Read Matthew 5:17-20, paying especially close attention to the key verse, Matthew 5:19.
- What emotions and attitudes do you think Matthew's use of hyperbole in this passage is meant to address?
- Do you think Jesus' use of "greatest" and "least" topples pride or incites pride? Is pride only negative all the time when it comes to bringing the kingdom of heaven to earth?

3. For Jesus, righteousness is not merely a personal thing. Our emotions, attitudes, and actions affect others. How do you feel about the following statement: "It's one thing to make decisions that might hurt ourselves, but it is something else all together, in fact flat out unacceptable, to teach others to do the same." Do you agree? Disagree?

SESSION THREE

Lutheran Context

For his whole life, Luther was seeking out how he could be in a "right relationship" (righteous) with God. This is what drove Luther to confession where his mentor chided him for being overly analytical about naming every single one of his sins. As a young monk, Luther got caught up in the "letter of the law" trying so hard to be righteous. Early on he would have eagerly taken up Matthew's challenge to "exceed in righteousness the scribes and Pharisees" who devoted their lives to studying and keeping the law.

1. What Jesus says in Matthew 5:20 is more than just some rhetorical device—it's a call to wisdom and grace.
- What are some ways we can get stuck trying so hard to follow a law that we forget the reason behind the law—for example, never eating dessert before dinner?
- Do you think heaven can come to earth if we simply work really hard at maintaining every religious law?
- How does Jesus' encounter with the Pharisees in Luke 11:37-44 add to our understanding of this?

2. What do you think Jesus' words, "I have come not to abolish, but to fulfill" mean in this context of righteousness? What additional understandings into this discussion do passages like Romans 3:21-26 and 2 Corinthians 5:18-20 provide?

In this text, Matthew is expressing high standards for those who are "justified." These high expectations include being more righteous than the scribes and Pharisees, being salt of the earth, and the light of the world.

3. Lutherans continue to have expectations for people living in the Christian community—expectations that start at their baptism and are affirmed as a part of their confirmation as active members in the church. What's included in the list of "expectations" from the service of "Affirmation of Baptism" as found in *Evangelical Lutheran Worship* (p. 236) or the *Lutheran Book of Worship* (p. 201)?

Notes

SESSION THREE

 Notes

Devotional Context

Even though we know that bringing heaven on earth is what Christians are to be about, we might feel too inadequate, too sinful, too unfamiliar with the Bible, to know how to make the kingdom of heaven a reality.

1. Think of someone you admire who taught you how to live for others. What qualities do you see in him or her? How do you think he or she got to be the person he or she is? Is he or she someone who overcame some odds?

It is nearly impossible to make daily decisions to follow someone or be a part of something if you do not understand them or believe in it. Before we can say we are willing to be salt, or light, the greatest, or even righteous before God, we need to understand as best as we can what we are saying yes to.

2. Read Ephesians 5:8-20 silently to yourselves. This is Paul's description of the "children of light." Focus on one aspect of this passage that you would like to turn up the dimmer switch on, something that would make you shine in ways that you haven't been shining. As you feel comfortable, share this with the group. As for being salt, how does Colossians 4:5-6 add to what it means to be a "seasoned" Christian?

3. Recap what you have learned so far and spend time talking about daily decisions that can help bring about heaven on earth.

Wrap-up

Be ready to look back over the work your group has done in this session.

Pray

Wise God, we thank you for choosing us, loving us just the way we are. We know we are not perfect, and yet we are capable. We have the ability to bring heaven to earth: to feed those who are hungry, provide shelter for those who are poor, give comfort to those who are lonely, and kindness to those who are grieving. Show us throughout this week how the decisions we make do change people's lives. In your holy name we pray. Amen.

SESSION THREE

Extending the Conversation

Homework

1. Read the next session's Bible text, Matthew 5:21-37, and come with thoughts and questions for conversation.

2. Look up 1 Corinthians chapters 12 and 13. Chapter 13 is often read in weddings as a way to love one other person. But in this text, Paul is speaking to Christian communities. Essentially he is asking them to live in such a way that would make manifest the kingdom of heaven. Reread chapter 13 verses 4-7 and add the words "in the kingdom of heaven" at the end of each phrase (for instance, "Love is patient in the kingdom of heaven . . ."). Knowing that every single person has a gift to offer, pray about how God might be using you and your gifts in particular to help bring about the kingdom of heaven.

3. There are many examples of "light" imagery in the Bible. Scripture also talks about God being present in the darkness. In a world where we use words like "white" and "black" to describe people's skin color, try to discover some ways in which God comes to us in both "the dark and the light." Share your observations with the group when you come back together.

4. Look at the baptismal liturgy in *Evangelical Lutheran Worship*. What does it say about light and candles? Think about real-life examples of how we might let our lights shine. Find your baptismal candle (or another special candle), light it, and say a prayer, asking God to help you let your light shine.

Enrichment

1. Jesus' teaching is chock full of figures of speech and rhetorical devices. Go online to find a list of rhetorical strategies such as this one: http://www.miracosta.edu/home/dperales/new rhetorical%20strategies.htm. Apply what you find on this list to the session text, or even to the Sermon on the Mount as a whole.

2. How important is it for Christians to rethink the language we use and in some instances the songs we sing, such as "Jesus Loves the Little Children" (Jesus loves the little children, all the children of the world, red and yellow, black and white . . .)? Try to come up with examples of language in well-known hymns and Christian songs that could be understood in negative ways.

3. Look up Luke 19:28-40. Then listen to the song by The Motor City Mass Choir, "Ain't Gonna Let No Rock" (http://music.

Notes

SESSION THREE

 Notes

myspace.com/index.cfm?fuseaction=music.artistalbums&artistid=14038401&albumid=12702774). Jesus was welcomed into Jerusalem because some understood him to be a king. Although he received a warm welcome, it was anything but a kingly processional (for example, he rode a donkey not a stallion). People were excited but didn't quite get what the kingdom of heaven was all about. But nothing will keep God from bringing heaven to earth—for even if we stop working towards it, the rocks will cry out! Think about how vital you are to God's goal of bringing heaven to earth.

For Further Reading

Read the quote by Marianne Williamson from her book, *A Return To Love: Reflections on the Principles of A Course in Miracles* (Harper Collins, 1992) from Chapter 7, Section 3 (pp. 190–191). Be encouraged that God uses all of us, human frailties and all, to bring heaven to earth.

> Our deepest fear is not that we are inadequate. Our deepest fear is that we are powerful beyond measure. It is our light, not our darkness that most frightens us. We ask ourselves, who am I to be brilliant, gorgeous, talented, fabulous? Actually, who are you not to be? You are a child of God. Your playing small does not serve the world. There is nothing enlightened about shrinking so that other people won't feel insecure around you. We are all meant to shine, as children do. We were born to make manifest the glory of God that is within us. It's not just in some of us; it's in everyone. And as we let our own light shine, we unconsciously give other people permission to do the same. As we are liberated from our own fear, our presence automatically liberates others.

Available at www.augsburgfortress.org/store:

God Reflected: Metaphors for Life by Flora A. Keshgegian (Fortress Press, 2008). Based on the traditional premise that everything we assert about God is metaphorical, this wonderfully written book presents a range of ways to imagine the nature of God and of God's power and will.

The Lutheran Handbook II (Augsburg Fortress, 2007). Never feel like you "don't know enough" Lutheran theology to accept a church council position or lead a Bible study! *The Lutheran Handbook II* puts it all at your fingertips.

SESSION FOUR

Matthew 5:21-37

Learner Session Guide

Focus Statement
Jesus invites us to perceive God's highest law: love comes first when heaven is a place on earth.

Key Verse
You have heard that it was said ... but I say to you ...
Matthew 5:21-22

If this is heaven on earth, what's up with all the laws?

Focus Image

Love changes everything. © Design Pics / SuperStock

Gather

Check-in
Welcome! Take this time to connect or reconnect with the others in your group. Be ready to share new thoughts or insights about your last session.

Pray
Jesus, we want to be faithful, but we know we aren't perfect. Guide our hearts and minds to hear what you are saying, that we may be careful to live it out. In your holy name we pray. Amen.

Focus Activity
Talk about some rules your family had growing up—for example the "two cookie" rule, the "pray before dinner" rule, or the "you must wear shoes outside" rule. What rules have you carried over to your adult or family life?

Session 4: Matthew 5:21-37   25

SESSION FOUR

 Notes

Open Scripture
Read Matthew 5:21-37.

- What were you glad to hear in this text? What is hard to hear in this text? Where there any surprises?

- Which of the four sections—anger, adultery, divorce, oaths—speak to you the most?

- Underline in your Bibles the words, "You have heard" and "But I say to you." Do Jesus' words, "But I say to you" change what "we have heard" or do they add to what we've heard?

Join the Conversation
Historical Context

Since almost all scholars regard the Gospel of Matthew as Jewish and since Jesus stayed close to his Jewish roots, it is understandable that the Sermon on the Mount would have Jesus expounding on what it meant to be a faithful Jew. Since "scholars agree that Matthew and his community are caught somewhere in the transitional process from Jewish sect to Christian religions" (*Fortress Introduction to the Gospels* by Mark Allan Powell [Fortress Press, 1998], p. 73), we see Jesus trying to bridge that gap.

1. Look at the following laws from the Pentateuch (the five books of Moses). Are they laws that we as Christians still live out today?
- Genesis 9:4-5
- Exodus 20:8
- Leviticus 19:19
- Numbers 18:25
- Deuteronomy 25:11-12

2. What is it about laws, even God's laws, that might cause our adherence to them to change over time? What wisdom does the apostle Paul in 1 Corinthians 3:4-6 inject into this discussion?

SESSION FOUR

A "great debate rages among scholars concerning the question of whether Matthew and his community still see themselves as belonging to Judaism." Are they more accurately described as "Jewish Christian" or "Christian Jews"? (*FIG*, p. 72)

3. Since Matthew's Gospel seems to flip-flop on both sides of this debate, at one time praising Judaism and the other showing distaste for rigid Pharisees, discuss how that might have made it difficult to find one's identity as an early Christian. Do transitional times remain difficult for Christians in the modern world? Discuss contemporary issues over which we struggle between the Spirit of the law versus the letter of the law.

Literary Context

In Matthew 13:52, Jesus considers his disciples to be like a "scribe who has been trained for the kingdom of heaven." The Gospel preachers and writers saw themselves as people who were rightly preserving and interpreting the good news of what God has been doing throughout time and uniquely now through Jesus.

1. Pay attention to the ways that Matthew works to offer direction for both preserving and interpreting this good news in a new light. What is both old and new about the "treasure" in each of the following verses? How would you apply these passages in the here and "now"?

- Matthew 5:21-26

    Old:_____

    New:_____

    Now:_____

- Matthew 5:27-30

    Old:_____

    New:_____

    Now:_____

- Matthew 5:31-32

    Old:_____

    New:_____

    Now:_____

- Matthew 5:33-37

    Old:_____

    New:_____

    Now:_____

Notes

SESSION FOUR

 Notes

2. Jesus believed that a true understanding of the Ten Commandments would help communities get along. Take some time to talk about the Focus Statement, especially the part about what it means to "perceive God's highest law." Then talk about the literary techniques of contrast and repetition in the phrase, "You have heard that it was said . . . but I say to you . . ."

- How many times does this phrase appear in Matthew 5?
- What does Jesus' use of it say about him and his message?
- How does Jesus' interpretation of these rules help to bring heaven on earth today?

Lutheran Context

Luther believed that "A Christian is a perfectly free lord of all, subject to none. A Christian is a perfectly dutiful servant of all, subject to all." Luther, and we as Lutherans, believe in the idea that we are both saints and sinners and for adhering to the doctrine of "both/and."

1. In today's Key Verse, we hear Jesus inviting us to dig deeper when it comes to living out "what we have heard."

- Why do you think Jesus makes "changes" to the law? Does Jesus in Matthew 5:21-37 place the commandments closer or further from our reach?
- How does Paul's view of the commandments in Colossians 2:8-23 relate to what you think Jesus is trying to teach in the Sermon on the Mount?

2. Ultimately Lutherans rely on something other than the application of God's law when it comes to realizing heaven on earth. How do Romans 7:21-25 and Galatians 2:19-21 speak to that reliance?

Lutherans believe that above all, God loves us. Baptizing infants is one way in which we outwardly express the belief that we can do nothing to deserve God's love, just as a child hasn't done a good work or believed rightly in order to receive God's promises. Yet Lutherans also understand that we respond to God's love by helping to bring about the kingdom of heaven right here on earth.

3. How easy or how hard is it to accept God's love for ourselves and others? Since human nature seems to be one of judgment, how can we uphold rules without judging?

SESSION FOUR

Devotional Context

Jesus' words in today's text may not seem very devotional at first. Few of us would probably open to Matthew 5:21-37 and choose to dwell upon these passages for inspiration. And yet this text is not as condemning as might be thought at first glance. In the same way our Focus Image is more complex than it may appear at first glance.

1. It might help to look at what these topics—anger, adultery, divorce, and vows—have in common. Why do you think Matthew/Jesus picked these topics, in particular, to expand upon with their original audience? How does it feel talking about these topics in church today?

2. Galatians 5:1, 13-14 reveals that faith in Jesus changes our relationship to God's laws from one of "slavery" to one of "freedom." What are some of the freedoms you are looking forward to in heaven? How can we live out our freedom in Christ here and now?

3. We often do not think of rules as heavenly, and yet it is God's commandments that guide and direct us to have heaven right here on earth. Think about "tough love" as characterized by setting boundaries and saying "no" for the best interests of the person being told "no." Look at how in these texts Jesus offers "tough love" to all of us. Talk about how "tough love" helps to create heaven on earth.

Wrap-up

Be ready to look over the work your group has done in this session.

Pray

God, as funny as it may sound, we thank you for your rules and laws, because they let us know how to live in relationship with you and each other. Help us to regularly engage in conversation about your laws, so that we might know how to live out heaven on earth. In Jesus' name. Amen.

Notes

SESSION FOUR

Notes

Extending the Conversation

Homework

1. Read the next session's Bible text: Matthew 5:38-48.

2. Jesus came "not to abolish the law" but to show us how to keep the law, and not just for law's sake, but for the sake of love—God's love for us and our love for others (Romans 13:8-10). Try to memorize "Love does no wrong to a neighbor; therefore love is the fulfilling of the law' (Romans 13:10) as a reminder of this.

3. Reflect on to Belinda Carlisle's pop hit "Heaven Is a Place on Earth" (MCA, 1987 http://www.youtube.com/watch?v=ng makCXGe7M). How do rules, for example monogamy, help human beings to experience love to the fullest sense?

4. Even though the Ten Commandments (Exodus 20:1-17) are primarily written in the negative (You shall not . . .), take a moment to rewrite them in the positive. This might help in recognizing how the commandments help us to live together as a community, thereby bringing heaven to earth.

Enrichment

1. Visit with your pastor about the value of vows, such as vows of confirmation, vows in court, or, perhaps, the vows that you made or heard in a wedding (*ELW*, p. 234 or p. 286). Discuss whether or not these vows help us to truly love. Why do you think Jesus warns us about making such vows in Matthew 5:33-37? Read also what Ecclesiastes 5:1-7 teaches about vows. What vow has God made with us through Christ? Check out 2 Corinthians 1:18-22!

2. A key concept for Lutherans is the idea of "law and gospel," where we live in a world of "both/ands." This does not mean Lutherans are "wishy-washy" but recognize the complexity of God and of our human nature. Recall a conversation with someone where you were pressed to state your faith in an either/or nature. Consider how you might now feel confident in sharing your faith in light of our understanding of "both/ands."

For Further Reading

The Year of Living Biblically: One Man's Humble Quest to Follow the Bible as Literally as Possible by A. J. Jacobs (Simon & Schuster, 2007). A self-admitted nominal Jew journals his attempt to keep all the commandments of the Bible over the course of a year, with results that waver between the ridiculous and the sublime.

SESSION FOUR

Available at www.augsburgfortress.org/store:

Fortress Introduction to the Gospels by Mark Allan Powell (Fortress Press, 1998). This is an excellent book to help understand the unique nature of each Gospel.

Check out http://www.elca.org/What-We-Believe/Social-Issues/Social-Statements.aspx. The way we live in community is different from when Matthew was writing this Gospel. Expectations for women, men, children, and families are different; for example, women are able to work outside the home, own property, get an education, and sign legal documents. In addition, family and community networks are vastly different from the tight communities of 1st century Palestine. Read the social statement on sexuality to see how the ELCA describes healthy marriage and sexual well-being today.

Notes

SESSION FIVE

Matthew 5:38-48

Learner Session Guide

Focus Statement
Creating heaven on earth isn't easy, but it's rewarding.

Key Verse
For if you love those who love you, what reward do you have? Matthew 5:46a

Bringing heaven to earth sounds hard—do we have what it takes?

 Focus Image

Holding up the peaceful promise of heaven on earth! © Design Pics / SuperStock

Gather

Check-in

Welcome! Take this time to connect or reconnect with the others in your group. Be ready to share new thoughts or insights about your last session.

Pray

Jesus, we are interested in heaven on earth. But to be honest, our lives are pretty full with jobs, family, and all kinds of responsibilities. It is a little daunting to think of being the kind of people you are calling us to be. Show us how we have what it takes to do both little and large things to make the kingdom of heaven a reality. Amen.

SESSION FIVE

Focus Activity

Think about the kinds of apologies that you've both given and received over the course of your lifetime.

- How often have you truly wanted to apologize to someone versus being forced to apologize (by a parent or a boss)?
- Have you been on the receiving end of someone's apology? Did their apology make a difference to you?
- How does it feel to try to get along with someone you don't like?

Open Scripture

Read Matthew 5:38-48.

> - What would be the hardest thing for you to do of all that Jesus teaches in today's session text? What would be the easiest?
>
> - What does the title "children of God" bring to mind? How does it make you feel?
>
> - In verse 45 we hear, "(God) makes his sun rise on the evil and on the good. . . ." Is this fair?

Join the Conversation

Historical Context

When asked to "love our enemies," our first thoughts might be of personal enemies: people who have gossiped about us, stolen from us, or treated us wrong in some way, shape, or form. Personal enemies were certainly a part of what Jesus was talking about, but he was also referring to religious groups that varied in their beliefs and oppressive groups. For Jesus' listeners, those two groups would have been the Samaritans, whose religious practices rivaled their own, and the Romans, who were controlling Judea as part of their vast empire.

1. Know your "enemy"!

- What does Luke 9:51-56 suggest about the Jews' relationship with the Samaritans?

 Notes

SESSION FIVE

- What does John 11:45-48 suggest about the Jews' relationship with the Romans?

2. Samaritans: The intense animosity between the Jews and the other inhabitants of Palestine is one that has roots reaching back to the days of Abraham and the rivalry between his two sons, Ishmael and Isaac. The Samaritans were a related people that settled into Jewish lands during the time of their Babylonian exile (598–538 B.C.E.). When the Jews returned from exile they found inhabitants who were closely related by blood, language and even worship practices, but who were not, strictly speaking, Jews. Conflict over all these matters persists to this day. Scan the following passages for the radical ways that Christians are to break this pattern of animosity.

- John 4:39-42
- Luke 10:29-37
- Luke 17:11-19

3. Romans: What began during the 400 years between the Old and New Testaments as an alliance between Jews and Romans to drive out the last of Alexander the Great's ruthless generals from Palestine became an opportunity for a total Roman domination of the eastern Mediterranean. The Jews were allowed some freedoms and even their own rulers, like Herod the Great and Herod Antipas, but they were merely puppets of Rome. The Roman legions and governors, like Pontius Pilate, were the true rulers in Judea, and the Jews hated that. How do the following passages reveal that Jesus advocates a different path than the rebellion-minded zealots of his day?

- Matthew 8:5:13
- Luke 13:1-5
- Mark 15:37-39

4. What do you think Jesus was hoping to accomplish in the minds of his listeners by not naming a specific enemy? How do his admonitions about radical love achieve heaven on earth?

Literary Context

Matthew continues to define love by how it plays out in community. In the first-century Mediterranean world, "love" and "hate" were understood more in terms of groups than individuals. Since people relied so much on their families and communities, how one was attached or unattached to their family or community made all the difference in the world. Here we see Jesus inviting those who have little power to use what power they have to shame their oppressors peacefully, yet publicly, to bring about positive change. The entire essence of the kingdom of heaven is in taking responsibility for each other's well-being—which takes place not when we seek revenge but when we invite the community to tell the aggressor their behavior is not okay.

1. Look at Matthew 5:43-44 in terms of this communal attachment: for example, "You have heard that it was said, 'You shall *be attached* to your neighbor and not *be attached* to your enemy.' But I say to you, *be attached* to your enemy and pray for those who persecute you. . . ." What do you hear when the text asks you to be "attached" to your enemy? What does this mean for how we get along as families, churches, neighborhoods, and governing bodies?

2. How do passages like Romans 12:14-21 and 1 Peter 1:12-19 expand on the radical principles of today's text, especially in regard to the careful use of shame and the value of community solidarity?

3. Matthew 5:38 is somewhat well known in pop culture ("an eye for an eye").
- How would you respond to someone saying that Jesus advocates taking revenge on the basis of this text?
- Why is reading this passage in the context of the verses around it so critical?

Lutheran Context

Liberation theology as taught in Lutheran circles means a "preferential option for the poor." In other words, Scripture shows us time and time again that God is interested in the "outsider," the widow, the orphan, the immigrant, the forgotten. The kingdom of heaven, therefore, is where all people, even the "evil," are welcome and allowed to live in the same amount of abundance as the next person—with health, education, shelter, comfort, companionship, and all the things that make us whole.

1. These texts use different examples to repeat over and over again God's generosity towards us. Whether we are "righteous" or "unrighteous," God gives us what we need. Is that fair?
- This being the case, why not live any way we want?
- Why love one's enemy when God seemingly loves and provides for everyone anyway?
- Bottom line—what's the value of "righteousness"?

Notes

SESSION FIVE

Notes

2. Discuss the joys and frustrations of everyone being recipients of God's love, especially in light of what Martin Luther writes in "The Freedom of a Christian." How do you feel about our role as love-givers as described in this quote and in the session text?

> From Christ the good things have flowed and are flowing into us . . . From us they flow on to those who have need of them so that I should lay before God my faith and my righteousness that they may cover and intercede for the sins of my neighbor which I take upon myself and so labor and serve them as if they were my very own. That is what Christ did for us. This is true love and the genuine rule of a Christian life. Love is true and genuine where there is true and genuine faith. Hence the Apostle says of love in I Cor. 13 [:5] that "it does not seek its own." (*Selected Writings of Martin Luther: 1520–1523*, Theodore G. Tappert, Ed. [Fortress Press, 2007], p. 47).

3. Our human nature makes it hard to accept God's lavish love when we often want people to "get what they deserve," whether that be the "good people" getting good things or the "bad people" getting bad things.

- In what ways does our session text speak against the notion that "you get what you deserve?"
- Read Luther's explanation to the First Article of the Apostles' Creed in the Small Catechism (*ELW*, p. 1162). What do we learn about God's motivations in this passage?
- How do God's motivations move us to bring the kingdom of heaven to earth?

Devotional Context

Jesus' words in the session Scripture text call us to give to those who have taken from us and love those who hurt us. Since Jesus gives us the example of healthy self-understanding, it would be incorrect to read into these verses that we should take abuse or unfair treatment by someone. Instead, these texts continue society's concern about honor/shame. By loving one's enemies, it is proving to the public that the "enemy" is the one to be shamed.

1. Wrestle with the ways we might misconstrue what Jesus is saying here and submit ourselves to harmful behavior, for example abusive relationships and codependence.

SESSION FIVE

 Notes

2. Many action movies are based on the idea of revenge, of hurting someone because of something they previously did to you.

- Can you name such a movie?
- Would you call this "justice" (as in the common phrase, "justice was served")?
- How can we understand justice differently, especially being mindful of those who are typically forgotten, neglected, or abused—those who are elderly, those who are poor, or immigrants? Are they given fair and equal treatment with those who have privilege and opportunity?
- How many movies can you name that give these kinds of "justice" themes? Why do you think there are more movies about revenge than justice?

Wrap-up

Be ready to look over the work your group has done in this session.

Pray

God, there is nothing like your love, and we are so grateful for how you pour it generously upon us. Help us to be mature enough to love others the way you love us. In Jesus' name we pray. Amen.

Extending the Conversation

Homework

1. Read the next session's Bible text: Matthew 6:24-34.

2. Presiding Bishop Mark Hanson speaks about faithfulness in the church as we find unity amidst our diversity. Find and read what he has to say at the following link:
http://www.elca.org/Who-We-Are/Our-Three-Expressions/Faithful-Mission.aspx

3. Read Mary Oliver's poem "What I Said at Her Service" from *Thirst* (Beacon Press, 2007). It was written upon the passing of Molly Malone Cook, to whom Oliver dedicates this volume. It is the shortest poem in the collection, but one that gives us great pause as to what perfection means. Discuss the poem with the group at your next gathering.

SESSION FIVE

4. Go through your own movie collection at home and make a list of all the movies you have that refer to revenge themes versus Jesus' sense of "justice" and heaven on earth.

Enrichment

1. Pray the newspaper this week. Using the daily newspaper in print or online, read an article each day and use it as a foundation for prayer.

2. Plan a "True Justice" film festival for the community that contrasts movies about revenge with those that provide a very different message—the gospel's message of heaven on earth. In addition to others you may have discussed, think about adding to the playbill movies like *Romero* (Paulist Pictures, 1989) about Catholic priest Oscar Romero from El Salvador. This movie is one of self-discovery, as a priest finds God leading him to be a voice for the poor in El Salvador, even at the risk of his own well-being. Other choices might include *Dead Man Walking* (Havoc, 1995) about a Catholic nun who offers spiritual care to a man on death row, and *The Power of Forgiveness* (First Run Features, 2009), which features spiritual leaders such as Elie Wiesel and Thich Nhat Hanh.

For Further Reading:

The ELCA has a strong justice and advocacy ministry which you can learn more about through this link: http://www.elca.org/Our-Faith-In-Action/Justice/Advocacy.aspx.

Available at www.augsburgfortress.org/store:

Selected Writings of Martin Luther, Theodore G. Tappert, ed. (Fortress Press, 2007). This collection includes the full variety of Luther's literary and religious writing: polemical and irenic, satirical and contemplative, academic and devotional.

SESSION SIX

Matthew 6:24-34

Learner Session Guide

Focus Statement

As Christians we first strive to make heaven on earth a reality, trusting that everything is ultimately in God's hands.

Key Verse

But strive first for the kingdom of God and his righteousness and all these things will be given to you as well. Matthew 6:33

Will you trust God for help in bringing heaven to earth?

Focus Image

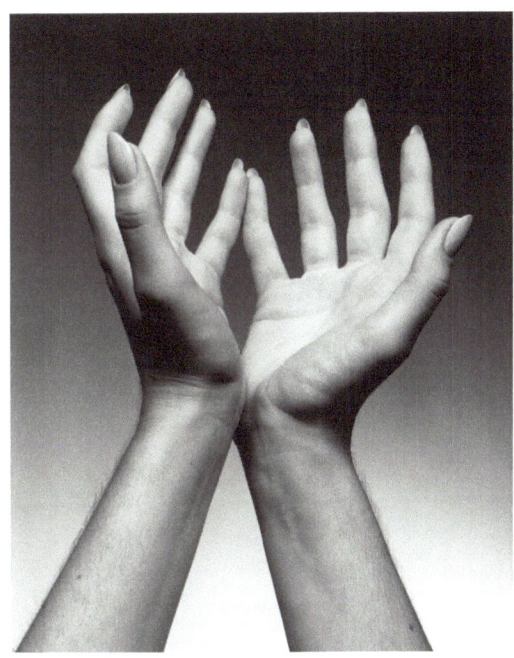

God's work. Our hands. © SuperStock / SuperStock

Gather

Check-in

Welcome! Take this time to connect or reconnect with the others in your group. Be ready to share new thoughts or insights about your last session.

Pray

God of new beginnings, there is nothing we do or say that is not a concern of yours. You care about us and are closer to us than we even know. Continue to plant in us a concern for bringing heaven to earth. Help us to release whatever worries us so that we can be open to what you would lay on our hearts. In Jesus' name we pray. Amen.

Focus Activity

What's the story behind the hands in the Focus Image? What kinds of thoughts and emotions might be on the mind of the person who is raising those hands? What are your hands stretching out

SESSION SIX

 Notes

for most right now; does it have anything to do with the "kingdom of heaven"? Pause silently for a few moments to compose your thoughts along these lines before sharing with the group.

Open Scripture
Read Matthew 6:24-34.

- Today's text does not ask if you give your heart to something, but what you give your heart to.

- What is the thing you will do anything for? What are "all these things" that will be given as mentioned in verse 33, after we seek God first?

- What life experiences have shaped your view of stuff?

Join the Conversation
Historical Context

Matthew's listeners were most likely common peasants who lived in the present moment concerned about their food, shelter and immediate needs from day to day. They were not in complete control of their material well-being, since the Romans were known for extracting heavy taxes to fund the empire by way of their Jewish tax collectors. Matthew was one of those hated tax collectors when he was called by Jesus to follow him (Matthew 9:9-13).

1. Read Matthew 6:24-34 as if you lived under the control of foreign invaders.
- If you were a Jew during the Roman occupation, how would these words sound to you?
- Does Jesus sound naïve about the realities of Jewish oppression? Or does Jesus provide hope amidst the worries, recognizing that being stuck in them only makes life worse?
- In what ways is verse 24 a bookend to verse 34? Chart the movement from slavery to freedom by way of the intervening verses.

SESSION SIX

2. Solomon was the son of David and a very wealthy and well-known king. Yet Solomon was not without troubles. In fact, he had so much to worry about that when asked what was the one thing he wanted, he asked for wisdom. No matter our socioeconomic status, we could all do with a little wisdom.

- Compare the wisdom of what you read in 2 Chronicles 9:22-28 with the philosophy attributed to Solomon in Ecclesiastes 2:18-26.
- How does Proverbs 15:16-17, from a section entitled "The Proverbs of Solomon," relate to today's session text?

Literary Context

The wisdom that Matthew provides is for us to seek God first; love God above all other things and live like you are bringing heaven to earth—then all these things God knows you need will be given to you as well.

1. Read Matthew 6:32. Matthew used the interchangeable phrase "kingdom of heaven/God" because it needed no explanation to the people of his day. Although "kingdom of heaven" is an important Christian concept, you may or may not be comfortable using this language to invite others to be a part of what God is doing in the world. Brainstorm other ways to refer to God's 21st century activities. Perhaps you can coin a contemporary phrase that conveys what you've learned about the "kingdom of heaven/God."

2. Jesus continues to use ordinary objects, as he did with salt and oil lamps, to talk about spiritual truths.
- What imagery does Jesus use in Matthew 6:24-34 to teach people about our lives in the "kingdom"?
- If you were telling someone how much God cares about them, which image would you use? Why?

Lutheran Context

God invites us continually to be cocreators. Therefore when it comes to the kingdom of heaven, we are collaborators in a divine work. Although God ultimately is the one who oversees our lives and places the desire in our heart for heaven to come to earth, it's our response to God's grace that makes the kingdom of heaven a reality.

1. Review the "Our Faith in Action" tab of the ELCA website (http://www.elca.org/Our-Faith-In-Action/Stories-of-Faith-in-Action.aspx) to find stories of striving for the kingdom of heaven.

Notes

SESSION SIX

 Notes

Which stories affect you most? What do they say about the priorities of the Evangelical Lutheran Church in America?

2. The kingdom of heaven is exciting. Like Mary's excitement in the "Magnificat" (Luke 1:46-55), it brings hopefulness to people as we anticipate what abundant life looks like for everyone. Lutherans still sing Mary's words in worship today. Look up hymns 234–236 in *Evangelical Lutheran Worship*. Compare these hymns of praise with Mary's prophetic words in Luke. List the ways they pronounce Jesus' role in bringing heaven to earth.

Devotional Context

The kingdom of heaven is not under sole ownership by the Christian church. God promises to work in and through the Christian community, but God is not limited by the church.

1. The word "economy" is formed from two Greek words that literally mean the "law" of the "home."
- How could the way you conduct your economic life set an example concerning not worrying?
- How might this spill over into your life outside the home? Outside the church?
- In what ways can our godly economics help bring about the kingdom of heaven?

2. Read Matthew 6:34. Jesus does not promise a worry-free life; rather, he acknowledges that life is full of worry and that worry is troublesome.
- Having learned in Session Five that God "makes his sun rise on the evil and on the good," what do you see are the advantages of being a Christian if it does not make the "good" better off than the "evil" or make one's life free of worry?
- How does Matthew 6:33 serve to refocus the energy that is often wasted on worry? Try to provide some local examples by which your group can strive beyond this study to bring heaven to earth.

Wrap-up

Be ready to look over the work your group has done in this session.

SESSION SIX

Pray

Alpha and Omega, God of the past, present, and future, we thank you for being with us on this journey. We pray for your continued wisdom in our lives as we become signs of the kingdom of heaven all around us. Most importantly, continue to search our hearts so that we may feel your Spirit tugging, guiding us to be instrumental in bringing heaven to earth. We love you. In Jesus' name we pray. Amen.

Extending the Conversation

Homework

1. Continue reading the entire book of Matthew, looking as you do for "signs of the kingdom" that you can bring near to earth today.

2. Read up on King Solomon in 1 Samuel Chapters 1–11.

3. If you haven't already, be sure to plan what your next Book of Faith conversation with God's Word is going to be. Go to www.bookoffaith.org to learn about the many opportunities to "extend" the conversation.

4. Track the local economics of the kingdom of heaven. How much of the average income of your members goes to your church? How much of the money from your church goes to fund the synod and church-wide ministries, including Lutheran camps and outreach missions that help to foster heaven on earth?

Enrichment

1. Lutherans are conscious that it is not just "right believing" but rightly living out what we believe that brings about heaven on earth. Look at the ELCA website http://www.elca.org/Our-Faith-In-Action/Responding-to-the-World.aspx and look through the various missions of the church. There are more Lutherans in Tanzania in Africa then there are currently in Germany in Europe, Martin Luther's home country. This is in large part due to the social activism of the Lutheran church that puts faith into action as participants in bringing heaven to earth.

2. Listen to U2's song "One," particularly the part about how we are to "carry each other." Bono, the front man for the rock band U2, has made a point of using his celebrity to help carry the needs of the voiceless to those who need to hear. Check out his ONE Campaign at www.ONE.org.

 Notes

SESSION SIX

 Notes

3. Many of us living in North America may not be as caught up with where our next meal is coming from, but we have no trouble finding things to be worried about. When you pray "Give us this day our daily bread" what kind of "daily bread" do you mean? Watch the movie *Food, Inc.* (Magnolia Pictures, 2008) to familiarize yourself with people who do have to worry about feeding their families with healthy affordable food.

4. The movie *God Grew Tired of Us* (High Point, 2006) is about Sudanese refugees seeking a better life. In it we see how we are all connected in this world and how every person can make a difference to help another out and bring heaven to earth.

For Further Reading:

Search for the Beloved Community: The Thinking of Martin Luther King Jr. by Kenneth L. Smith and IRA G. Zepp (Judson Press, 1998). A condensed article on this treatise about being a community that helps God's kingdom come can also be found here: http://www.religion-online.org/showarticle.asp?title=1603.

Gospel of Thomas, Sayings 36 and 47 (http://www.sacred-texts.com/chr/thomas.htm). Compare this Gnostic text with what we read in today's session text.

Available at www.augsburgfortress.org/store:

Sustaining Simplicity: A Journal by Anne Basye (Augsburg Fortress, 2007). The book is an honest, in-depth sharing of the successes and struggles of one person facing down world-consuming materialism as she lives joyfully and justly.

Shaking the Gates of Hell: Faith-Led Resistance to Corporate Globalization by Sharon Delgado (Fortress Press, 2007). This book proposes a way for people of faith to respond to the growing power of corporations and their domination of the world's cultures, governments, and global institutions.

www.ingramcontent.com/pod-product-compliance
Lightning Source LLC
Chambersburg PA
CBHW041117070526
44584CB00002B/200